This Book Belongs To:

_____

C·Z· GUEST'S
5 SEASONS OF GARDENING
Planner

C·Z·GUEST
Photographs by Elvin McDonald

A BULFINCH PRESS BOOK

Little, Brown and Company • Boston • New York • Toronto • London

First Edition

Library of Congress Cataloging-in-Publication Data
Guest, C. Z. [5 seasons of gardening planner]
C. Z. Guest's 5 seasons of gardening planner / C. Z. Guest ; photographs by Elvin McDonald. — 1st ed.
p.   cm.
"Portions of this text were originally published in C.Z. and Elvin's week by week garden guide" — T.p. verso.
"A Bulfinch Press book."
ISBN 0-8212-2039-X
1. Gardening.   2. Gardening — Calendars.   I. McDonald, Elvin.   II. Title.
III. Title: C. Z. Guest's five seasons of gardening planner.   IV. Title: 5 seasons of gardening planner.
SB453.G873 1994
635 — dc20   93-26354

Bulfinch Press is an imprint and trademark of Little, Brown and Company (Inc.)
Published simultaneously in Canada by Little, Brown & Company (Canada) Limited

Designed by Martine Bruel

PRINTED IN SINGAPORE

Dear Reader:

If you've read my book *C. Z. Guest's 5 Seasons of Gardening,* you'll know that I am a demon for organization. So, it made perfect sense to make my next project a new yearly garden planner and organizer. I recreated this planner for myself: a single calendar that combines all the quick reference material that I use, plus gardening tips and everyday information that gardeners need.

This new garden organizer will enable you to chart the plants in your garden through the year, from sowing and fertilizing to cultivation, blooming, and harvest. I've added information and advice based on my experiences in the garden at "Templeton" (my Long Island house). If you've read my book you'll be able to organize your year into the five seasons of gardening. As we all know, the final season of gardening is the holiday season, my favorite.

In addition to holiday tips, you'll find in the following pages seed productivity charts, a list of bulbs and when to plant them, and a table of the most compatible "bedmates." There are also four separate garden diagrams, so you can plan out your bulb and flower beds, vegetable garden, and landscape plans, or use them to show what crops your garden will yield in three successive plantings.

In creating this garden planner, my desire is to make your life easier. First and foremost I hope you use this planner to organize your garden. After that I hope you can get pleasure and help from the information, tips, charts, and diagrams to make your garden more productive and beautiful than ever.

Best of luck—happy gardening.

C. Z. Guest

JANUARY

*J*ANUARY is winter inspection time. Harsh winter weather—ice and wind—can damage trees and shrubs, and it's your job to check the yard after each storm. Make sure that the plants you've protected with burlap are still secure in their wrappings. If any branches have been broken off the trees, clean up the debris and be sure to remember the spot when it comes time for spring doctoring.

This month, waste not, want not is the rule. Save the wood ashes from your fireplace to spread around fruit trees, peonies, roses, lilacs, and delphiniums in the spring. The ashes contain potash, calcium, and phosphoric acid and serve as a natural fertilizer and soil conditioner. Save branches from your Christmas tree to blanket bulb beds and rock gardens.

Indoors, houseplants that are resting should be kept damp and without fertilizer—it's good for their diets. Pinch off yellow leaves, since new ones are on the way. Winter heating dries your skin, and it also causes dryness in your plants, a *big* problem during the winter in most apartments and houses. To increase humidity, place trays filled with pebbles and water under your plants and mist often. Group moisture-loving plants in the same room and operate a humidifier for them.

During the winter months, be sure to feed the birds. Food insulates their little bodies and helps them stay warm. Also, remember that birds get thirsty; water freezes less quickly in a wooden or clay bowl, or add a drop of glycerine to your birdbath. A mirror placed in the bottom of your birdbath will also help it stay warm.

Get ready!

Gardenias and anisodonteas

A statue made by the French sculptor Coysevox in 1710. It was given to my mother-in-law by her father in 1910.

Tips.
Gently remove snow that piles on branches of small trees and evergreens. Wet, icy snow can be heavy for tender limbs and cause plant injury. Send for free seed catalogs now. A postcard will bring you a catalog that is a virtual textbook on vegetable, fruit, and flower varieties. (See the list at the end of this planner for the names and addresses of some mail-order seed suppliers.) Substitute coarse sand or wood ash for rock salt on frozen walkways to protect adjacent plants from salt injury. And stay off the grass—it's easily damaged this time of year. Think about last year's successes and failures, and take the time to learn about basic gardening problems that concerned you during the past growing season.

Cold Frames.
With the help of a cold frame, easily made at home, it is possible to extend greatly the growing season of your garden. Use it in the spring to give seedlings a head start, away from the evening chill; in the winter it will help protect late crops and force flowering bulbs.

A cold frame is nothing more than a bottomless box with a hinged, light-admitting lid that can be closed to keep out the cold. To make a base for the cold frame, cut exterior-grade plywood and assemble the pieces with removable-pin hinges. For the cover, fasten lengths of lumber into angle irons, paint the entire box, and wrap clear polyethylene sheeting over the top and secure with heavy staples. On frosty evenings, cover the frame with 8 to 10 inches of hay for added insulation. On hot days open the frame and let your plants breathe.

PLANT	DATE PLANTED	COMMENTS

Beets and parsley

F EBRUARY'S dreary days can be brightened by forcing out-of-season plants and flowers. Forsythia, pussy willow, apple, plum, and peach branches are all good candidates and bring impatient gardeners a promise of spring.

Visit garden nurseries now to see what's available for early planting. Asparagus roots, onion sets, and strawberry plants come in about now. And if you're lucky enough to have a greenhouse or cold frame you should start your seedlings and cuttings — flowering annuals, beets, tomatoes, celery, leeks, lettuce, and onions are good choices — so you'll have a head start on outdoor planting when the threat of frost is over. Keep a fan going in the greenhouse after seedlings begin to poke through the soil, to keep plants from damping off or developing mildew. And place fluorescent lights only about 6–8 inches directly above seedlings so they'll grow stocky.

Tips.

Scoop up some nice clean snow, let it melt, and use it for watering your plants. Snow contains wonderful minerals — mainly nitrogen — although in some areas it may be somewhat acid. 🐛 A once-weekly watering with weak tea is a good tonic for ferns. 🐛 Recipe for a dandy indoor soil mix: two parts potting soil, one part coarse sand, and one part compost, plus a tablespoon or two of bonemeal per peck (8-quart dry measure) of mix. 🐛 You can get a good germination from most seeds by starting them in plastic foam coffee cups filled with a sterile potting soil. Water and then place a clear plastic tumbler over each cup, so you can see when the seeds sprout. Harden them off slowly by propping up the cover. 🐛 Yearly pruning of fruit trees, especially apples, should be done now through mid-March. When you prune, be sure to keep away from "bleeder" trees (the trunk leaks valuable sap when you cut it) like maple, beech, dogwood, elm, and sycamore. Wait until they come into full leaf later this spring. 🐛

Tomatoes

Primula polyanthus Primrose

Set branches of quince, forsythia, and crab apple in large vases filled with lukewarm water in a cool, well-lit, but not sunny room. In a few weeks you'll have a beautiful display of spring finery.

Compatible "Bedmates." Scientists can't explain it, but experienced gardeners have found that certain planting combinations actually enhance growth and reduce insect troubles. Keep these combinations in mind when ordering your seeds this month and next. Here are some to try:

Flowering almond branch

ASPARAGUS, basil, parsley, tomatoes
BEANS, marigold, celery, potatoes
BEETS, carrots, onions, kohlrabi, cauliflower, kale, broccoli, brussels sprouts, turnips, cabbage
CARROTS, onions and parsley (which repel carrot fly), beets, peas, sage
CORN, beans, cucumbers, lettuce, soybeans (to repel chinch bugs), spinach, squash
CUCUMBERS, corn, radishes (to repel cucumber beetles)
LETTUCE, cabbage, onions, radishes
NASTURTIUMS, potatoes, squash
ONIONS, carrots, lettuce, radishes
PEAS, beans, carrots, corn, potatoes, turnips
PEPPERS, carrots, eggplants, onions, tomatoes
POTATOES, corn, eggplants, peas
RADISHES, carrots, lettuce, spinach
SQUASH, beans, corn, radishes
STRAWBERRIES, borage, lettuce, spinach
TOMATOES, marigolds (which cut nematode

populations), spinach, carrots, mint, lettuce, basil, nasturtiums
TURNIPS, peas

Incompatible species, that simply *cannot* get along!

ASPARAGUS, onions, garlic
BEANS, onions, garlic, shallots, gladiolus
BEETS, pole beans
BRASSICAS, tomatoes, strawberries
CARROTS, dill
CORN, tomatoes (the corn earworm will damage both, if it can!)
CUCUMBERS, potatoes, all aromatic herbs
ONIONS, pole beans, peas, beans
PEAS, shallots, garlic, onions
POTATOES, tomatoes, sunflowers
MOST SPECIES, fennel, sunflowers, walnut trees
—all known to inhibit growth of nearby plants

PLANT	DATE PLANTED	COMMENTS

Lilies, tulips, and foxglove

$\mathcal{M}$ARCH is the time to start thinking about your garden and planning for best results. A workable garden plan includes a list of crops to plant, varieties to select, the amount of seeds, or number of seedlings needed, planting dates, and the location and spacing of each crop. It's often helpful to work up a diagram of just how every inch of space in your garden will be used.

Consider carefully the location of your garden. Does it get enough sun? (Six hours a day is the very least most plants require.) Will the garden drain properly? Is the space convenient to a watering source? These are all important questions to keep in mind when mapping out a new garden site.

Next consider the soil. The spring weather may have left the earth too damp and cold to work (try squeezing a handful of soil; it should crumble apart rather than clump damply). In many areas of the country March is too early for planting, but if you're lucky you may be able to sow an early planting of cool-weather crops that can withstand the occasional dips in temperature.

Whatever area you live in, you can probably begin planting lettuce, radishes, and peas now, and start peppers, tomatoes, eggplants, celery, broccoli, and cauliflower in the cold frame or greenhouse. It's time to start many annuals (under lights) as well, including asters, phlox, snapdragons, ageratum, and nicotiana.

Spring thaws can be dangerous to shrubs and bushes as the tops begin to shed water that their frozen roots can't replace. To prevent dehydration, try to keep them shaded with burlap until the ground is completely thawed.

Pelargonium domesticum

Snowdrops

Camellia

Tips.
Don't forget to complete any pruning still to be done on fruit trees. Dormant spraying—horticultural spray oils applied anytime prior to bud "break"—is an excellent way to control many insect and mite pests on trees and shrubs. Always spray on a windless day. Now that the soil has started to warm up, begin moving or transplanting trees and shrubs. For those perennials already up a few inches, spread a ring of fertilizer around them and water. Azaleas, cyclamen, mums, and other gift plants can have prolonged blooming periods if put in a cool room (50°F) at night. As temperatures rise, gradually uncover, prune, and feed established roses. If you're lucky enough to have red raspberry bushes, they need attention now. Cut out old fruiting canes, thin out the weaker new canes, and remove the upper 12 inches of the remaining canes. This is an excellent time to put down the first application of an inorganic lawn fertilizer. By the end of this month you may be able to remove some of the mulch or winter protection from flower beds, depending on the temperatures in your area. Wait about 2 to 3 weeks to take off the rest. Now is a good time to fertilize shade trees and evergreens if this wasn't done last fall.

PLANT	DATE PLANTED	COMMENTS

'Fire Dancer' geranium

PLANT	DATE PLANTED	COMMENTS

PLANT	DATE PLANTED	COMMENTS

Mandevilla or dipladenia
'Red Riding Hood' and
pink hybrid geraniums

APRIL is a month of hope and anticipation, when the first signs of the renewal of life that means spring become visible. I'm always so excited to see the bulbs I planted the previous fall pushing their noses out of the ground. Every day brings a new surprise, with not only plants but the birds and animals putting in their appearances too.

This month begins with still-chilly temperatures, and although you can expect warmer weather by month's end, you should never plant until the frost is completely out of the soil, or your seeds won't germinate. To encourage the soil to warm up, pull all mulches back from the planting bed; bare soil warms up more quickly. Prepare the soil in the vegetable garden and annual beds, adding lime only if needed. (Have your state agricultural extension service test your soil's pH, or potential of hydrogen—a measure of acidity or alkalinity. They will do this for a small fee. Allow at least four weeks if you send your specimen in the spring.)

Seedlings coming along in cold frames need special attention now. Keep the sash closed while temperatures remain below freezing and gradually harden them off by letting in some air (on the side away from the wind) once the temperature is above 32°F. And remember, it's still too chilly outdoors in most of the northern latitudes for houseplants—keep them inside until May 15. Who needs a cold? Certainly not our plants —and a sudden change in climate can be harmful to their health.

Do plant or sow plenty of cool-weather crops, such as beets, broccoli, cabbage, cauliflower, lettuce, onions, and sugar snap peas, all through this month.

Easter cactus

Prunus pilosiuscula

Tips.

An organic mulch, especially one containing a variety of plant materials such as peat moss, salt hay, grass clippings, and shredded oak leaves, will supply mature or near-mature trees and shrubs with the proper nutrients for health, color, and vigor. ❧ Shrubs and trees need less fertilizer than young plants for which accelerated growth is needed. Evergreens need less fertilizer than deciduous plants. ❧ Street trees, which are exposed to pollutants and stress through restricted root growing, need more nutrients than garden or lawn trees. ❧ Cutworms are a menace to newly set-out vegetable plants. Here's what I do, using recycled materials to protect seedlings from invasion. Take the tops and bottoms off dog food or tuna fish cans, wash and dry them, and put one can over each plant. Once the plants are well established, remove the cans and store for the next spring. ❧ Continue planting herbaceous perennials throughout April, and divide established ones before growth is too far advanced. ❧ Be sure to prune early-flowering shrubs immediately after flowering. Finish the pruning of deciduous trees and shrubs and roses before new growth begins.

Pollination of Fruit Trees.

Pollination is an aspect of growth that nature takes care of so efficiently herself that most gardeners never give it a thought, allowing honeybees, bumblebees, and the spring breezes to do all the work. Simply put, pollination is the transfer of pollen from the anthers to the pistil of a plant, and, of course, it is essential for fruit production. Some trees will not set fruit when fertilized only with pollen from their own blossoms. These varieties are not self-fruitful and must be planted close to a different variety, which provides the pollen. Self-fruitful trees will bear fruit even if planted by themselves, but better fruit set will always occur if additional trees are nearby to ensure a proper supply of pollen. Fortunately, nature sees to most of the details, but you can give her a boost by planting your fruit trees with pollination in mind.

Planting for Pollination

Figs

APPLES: Most varieties are self-sterile or self-unfruitful. Plant two varieties.

APRICOTS: Self-fruitful.

BLACKBERRIES and RASPBERRIES: Self-fruitful.

BLUEBERRIES: Self-fruitful but better results occur with cross-pollination.

CHERRIES (bush): Self-unfruitful. Plant two varieties.

CHERRIES (pie): Self-fruitful.

CHERRIES (sweet): Self-unfruitful. Plant Black Tatarian with Golden Sweet. Montmorency pie cherries will pollinate Kansas sweet cherries. Stella is self-fruitful.

CURRANTS and GOOSEBERRIES: Self-fruitful.

FIGS: Self-fruitful.

GRAPES: Self-fruitful.

HAZELNUTS and CHINESE CHESTNUTS: Self-unfruitful. Plant two varieties.

NECTARINES: Self-fruitful.

NUTS, most varieties: Self-fruitful.

PAPAWS: Self-fruitful.

PEACHES: Self-fruitful.

PEARS: Self-unfruitful. Plant two varieties. (Bartlett and Seckel will not pollinate each other.)

PERSIMMONS: Self-unfruitful. Plant both male and female persimmon trees.

PLUMS (common): Self-unfruitful. Plant two varieties.

PLUMS (European type): Self-fruitful.

STRAWBERRIES: Self-fruitful.

PLANT	DATE PLANTED	COMMENTS

PLANT	DATE PLANTED	COMMENTS

Lettuce, carrots, beets,
cabbage, corn

PLANT	DATE PLANTED	COMMENTS

PLANT	DATE PLANTED	COMMENTS

Purple sage

Planting Diagram: It is time to plant your annuals—calendula, cosmos, and marigolds, for example.

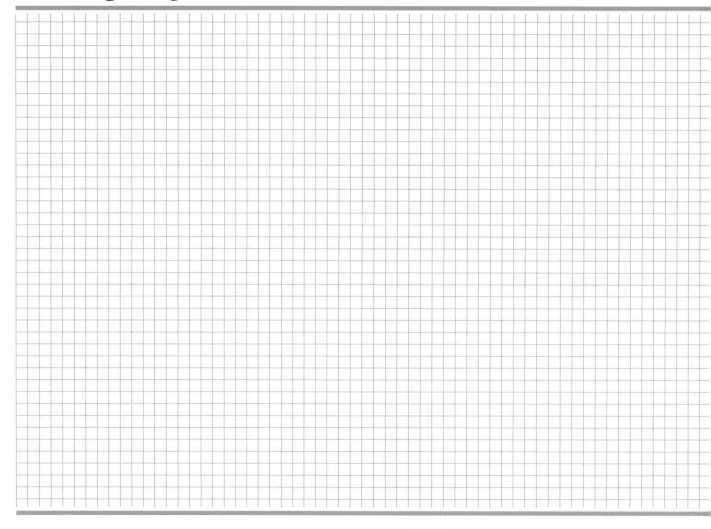

Your first salad garden of the year can go in now, along with herbs such as basil, rosemary, parsley, and tarragon.

Dutch iris

$\mathcal{M}$AY is the busiest month of the year for a gardener. There's lots to be done, and you'll have to hurry to keep pace with nature. With the coolest weather of spring just past and the steamy summer heat still to come, plants are budding, birds are singing, animals are scurrying, and you're busy planting, fertilizing, pruning, and checking to make sure that every nook and cranny of your planting space is hard at work. The only damper on this fabulous spring feeling is that sometimes Mother Nature can play a terrible trick. Don't be too disappointed if there's a mid-May slowdown in the garden owing to "unseasonably" chilly temperatures.

May means lilies of the valley, iris, peonies, and azaleas, followed by lilacs and late tulips. All your perennials are shooting up to meet the spring sun. You can also start planting forget-me-nots, lobelia, nasturtiums, and vinca, even if the soil is a bit wet.

In the vegetable garden it's time to sow chives, rutabagas, beets, parsnips, carrots, parsley, Swiss chard, turnips (for an early crop), and mustard greens; a bit later in the month you can add cucumber, corn, cantaloupe, pole beans, okra, basil, squash, dill, pumpkins, and New Zealand spinach to your crop. If you've sown your favorite vegetables by the third week of this month, you'll be eating well by July! And that's the most rewarding thing about this month—you'll see all your time and hard work pay off soon.

Lilacs

Iceland poppies

Tips.

Spray your deciduous trees with Bt *(Bacillus thuringiensis)* formula now only if you had a gypsy moth problem last year. If you had no gypsy moth problem, don't worry this year. 🌿 Tilling and plowing in the spring and fall are essential, as they bring weed seeds to the top of the soil surface, where they sprout fast and die. Weeds are easily controlled when they're young and don't have a strong foothold in your garden, but once established, look out! 🌿 If you have trouble getting geraniums to bloom properly, it may be they are not pot-bound; that is, the roots have not yet taken all the available space, becoming a bit stressed. This condition *must* exist before the plants will put on a good show. 🌿 Plant sunflowers near your peas to cut down on your aphid problems. Aphids that venture near the sunflowers will stick to the underside of the leaves like flies to flypaper. 🌿 When mulching trees, don't pack the mulch against the trunk. Spread the mulch away from the base, leaving a space of 3 to 6 inches between the trunk and the mulch. 🌿 It's time to take another look at your roses to make sure all the dead canes have been cut out. May is the month to fertilize your roses. I think the very best fertilizer is bonemeal. 🌿 Watch out for cross-pollination if you grow both sweet corn and popcorn. Put plenty of room between the two varieties, or plant a row of sunflowers around the corn patches, so drifting pollen will be caught on the flowers' tiny sticky hairs.

Seed Sense.

Sometimes starting your garden from seed, rather than seed-lings, can be confusing. How much should be planted, and when? This is a general guideline for planting 25-foot garden rows. If you have a smaller (or larger—good for you!) space to cultivate, divide (or multiply) accordingly. Check seed packages for seed-depth, row spacing, and thinning instructions. Of course, maturing dates are approximate, and will vary according to the zone you live in.

Vegetable Planting Chart

VEGETABLE	SOW	WHEN TO PLANT	DAYS TO MATURITY	APPROXIMATE YIELD
Asparagus	1 packet	Spring	3–4 Years	8 lbs.
Beans, bush	¼ lb.	April-August	50–60	½ bushel
Beans, pole	¼ lb.	May-June	60–70	½ bushel
Beets	1 packet	March-August	50–70	½ bushel
Brussels sprouts	⅛ oz.	April-July	70–130	8 quarts
Cabbage, early	¼ oz.	April-July	60–90	37 lbs.
Carrots	1 packet	March-July	60–80	½ bushel
Cauliflower	1 packet	April-July	55–60	15 heads
Cucumbers	1 packet	May-July	50–80	25 lbs.
Eggplants	1 packet	May-June	75–90	30 fruits
Endive	1 packet	April-July	60–90	25 lbs.
Kale	½ packet	April-July	50–80	1 bushel
Kohlrabi	1 packet	April-July	50–80	20 lbs.
Lettuce, leaf	1 packet	March-September	40–60	18 lbs.
Onion, seeds	1 packet	March-May	100–150	½ bushel
Parsnips	½ packet	March-May	90–150	½ bushel
Peas	¼ lb.	March-May	55–90	½ bushel
Peppers	½ packet	May-June	60–80	75 fruits
Potatoes	25 sets	March-June	80–120	1 bushel
Pumpkins	1 packet	May-June	70–120	23 fruits
Radishes	1 packet	March-September	20–60	25 lbs.
Rhubarb	13 roots	Spring	2 years	125 stalks
Rutabagas	1 packet	June-July	80–95	25 lbs.
Spinach	1 packet	August-November	40–70	2 lbs.
Squash, winter	1 packet	May-June	80–120	15 fruits
Swiss chard	½ packet	March-June	55–65	17 lbs.
Tomatoes	1 packet	May-June	55–90	1½ bushels
Turnips	1 packet	July-August	30–60	½ bushel

Tulips

PLANT	DATE PLANTED	COMMENTS

Hydrangeas

Geranium

PLANT	DATE PLANTED	COMMENTS

PLANT	DATE PLANTED	COMMENTS

Chinese hibiscus

PLANT	DATE PLANTED	COMMENTS

Rothschild azaleas

PLANT	DATE PLANTED	COMMENTS

Iceland poppies

PLANT	DATE PLANTED	COMMENTS

Japanese herbaceous peony

Planting Diagram: Your vegetable garden will dominate this planting period. Tomato plants, squash,

melons, cucumber, eggplant, and peppers should all be planted. Flowers such as zinnias and cleome are ready to go as well.

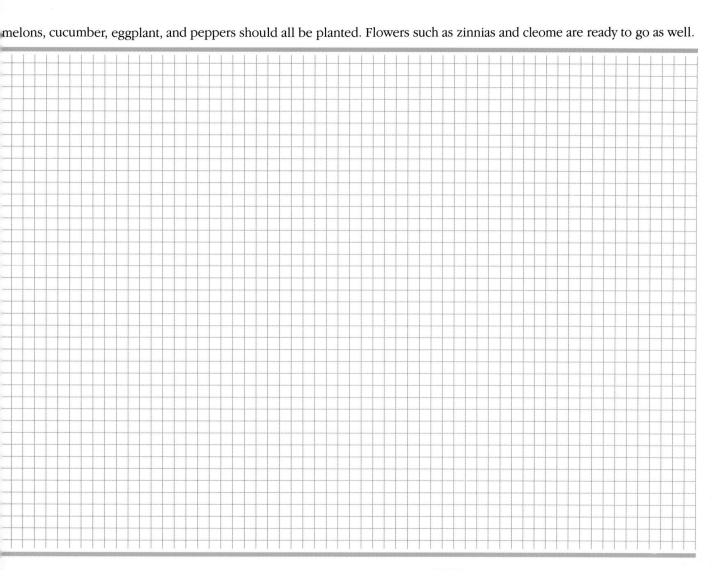

*J*UNE signals the end of chilly evening temperatures in most areas, and potted plants and flowers can now safely be brought outdoors (when night temperatures are over 60°F) to adorn patio and yard.

There should be plenty of activity in the vegetable garden by now, with some of the early-spring plantings of cool-weather crops—lettuce, peas, beans, radishes, broccoli, carrots, and beets—ready to eat. As the temperatures climb, be sure to sow new seed plantings deeper than in previous months to protect them from the harsh summer sun. And the time is right now to put in seedlings of warm-weather crops such as squash, peppers, and eggplants.

As your flowering plants come into full bloom, remember to give them attention. Like June itself, perennials return faithfully year after year; with a minimum of care and a small initial investment, you can have a glorious garden that will flower forever. I recommend buying plants because the seed for perennials takes a long time to grow to blooming size. A beautiful garden (no matter what scale) will give you an enormous sense of pride and accomplishment. But remember, your garden is never finished.

Freesia

East Friesland hardy salvia

Tips.

Asparagus should be cut before June 20. Later cutting tends to weaken the roots and consequently makes the crop smaller the next year. 🌱 Evergreens should not be pruned after mid-July because the new growth will be unable to harden off before winter. 🌱 Broccoli can be harvested over a long season (from planting time) because once the larger center head is cut, side shoots will develop into small clusters. Always harvest broccoli before the yellow flowers open. 🌱 If cloudy or wet weather is tough on your melons, eggplants, sweet corn, or pole limas, compensate by planting more carrots, beets, and greens, with a narrow strip of sand on top of the soil to hasten germination. 🌱 Take seed pods off early-blooming shrubs such as mock orange, lilac, and rhododendron. Prune any overgrown specimens. Feed them if they have not been previously fed, and give an ample dressing of compost and mulch to all ornamental shrubs and trees. 🌱 Japanese beetles are due this month. Using white hollyhocks as lures, handpick early arrivals in the morning while the dew still hampers their normal swift takeoff.

Peonies

Digitalis mertonensis

PLANT	DATE PLANTED	COMMENTS

PLANT	DATE PLANTED	COMMENTS

Daisies and columbines

PLANT	DATE PLANTED	COMMENTS

Coreopsis grandiflora
'Sunray'

PLANT	DATE PLANTED	COMMENTS

Lavender

Platycodon

PLANT	DATE PLANTED	COMMENTS

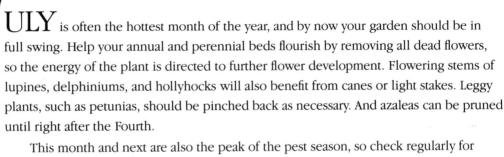

JULY is often the hottest month of the year, and by now your garden should be in full swing. Help your annual and perennial beds flourish by removing all dead flowers, so the energy of the plant is directed to further flower development. Flowering stems of lupines, delphiniums, and hollyhocks will also benefit from canes or light stakes. Leggy plants, such as petunias, should be pinched back as necessary. And azaleas can be pruned until right after the Fourth.

This month and next are also the peak of the pest season, so check regularly for insect and disease problems. Don't let them get ahead of you. Treat as needed, handpick if possible, and use only insecticidal soap spray. No chemicals!

Try these homegrown, hazard-free insect repellents: pungent onion skins to drive beetles away from squash and cucumber plants; dill and borage to help repel hornworms from tomato territory; and soybeans planted around corn patches to lure any furry four-footed animal invaders away from your crop. Nasturtiums, marigolds, and mustard also rebuff numerous gnawing pests with their color and pungent aroma.

If the soil in your garden is showing the effects of heavy producing, add nutrients before planting some of the cold-weather crops. You will have a more plentiful harvest come the end of summer (and warm weather) in late August and September.

Hardy lilies

Peppers

Tips.

Mulching and weeding go hand in hand, as both are essential to conserving moisture. Place a 1- to 2-inch layer of mulch around each baby plant and pull weeds regularly. 🐛 After summer heat breaks, plant biennials such as pansies, foxgloves, Sweet William, and wallflower. 🐛 Water is the most crucial part of late-summer gardening. In very dry, hot weather you may have to treat your garden to a fine spray of water several times a day until seeds have germinated—two weeks or so. Use a fine spray to avoid dislodging tiny seeds. 🐛 The fruit of the rosebush, the rose hip, makes a wonderful tea. If the hips are large (such as from *Rosa rugosa*) cut them in half, otherwise steep whole in boiling water for 5 to 10 minutes and strain. 🐛 My Bug Juice Cocktail: If pests are attacking your crops, grind up a few of the offending insects in your blender with a little water. Dilute this solution and spray it back on the crops. It works! 🐛 Heat may cause garden soil to crust over, making it impossible for seedlings to push aboveground, so cover newly planted rows with sand. 🐛 Inspect and maintain houseplants that have been moved outdoors for the summer. Move them to a more protected location if they're exposed to too much sun. 🐛 Prune climbing roses after flowering to promote new growth, and apply a summer mulch to all roses. 🐛 Do not fertilize woody plants after July 1; it promotes tender late-season growth that will be subject to winterkill. 🐛 Many deciduous trees, especially sycamores and London planes, drop up to 10 percent of their leaves during hot, dry weather. This is part of the trees' strategy to conserve water and is not harmful.

Allium giganteum

PLANT	DATE PLANTED	COMMENTS

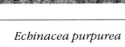

Echinacea purpurea

Sunflower

PLANT	DATE PLANTED	COMMENTS

PLANT	DATE PLANTED	COMMENTS

Pattypan squash

PLANT	DATE PLANTED	COMMENTS

Capsicum annuum

PLANT	DATE PLANTED	COMMENTS

Tithonia Mexican sunflower

*A*UGUST is a bounteous time in the garden, and yours should be glorious with roses, lilies, hollyhocks, zinnias, marigolds, and asters, and bursting with beans, beets, corn, melons, onions, potatoes, squash, and tomatoes ready for harvest. Extend the growing season of your vegetable beds by succession planting cool-weather crops like beans, endive, peas, spinach, radishes, and lettuce. You may also want to preserve your garden harvest by canning or freezing some of your overstock.

This is a good time to plant, divide, or move your irises, tulips, or other bulb plants, and order bulbs such as freesias, paper-white narcissus, and ranunculus for forcing during the holiday season. Make geranium cuttings from your healthiest plants to guarantee a generation of vigorous youngsters. Cut out raspberry and blackberry canes that have just fruited, but resist the temptation to fertilize or prune your trees and shrubs now; it's too late in the season for them to begin another growth spurt before the onset of autumn.

Topiary yew tree and hedges

Gloriosa daisy and Summer
Pastels achillea

Tips.

Cauliflower cannot stand as much cold as cabbage and won't head up properly in hot weather. When the head starts to develop, tie the leaves together over the curd so that it turns milky white.  The mealybug's white, waxy covering protects it from many pesticides, but home gardeners can control these pests by spraying with a 50-percent solution of water and alcohol (rubbing alcohol will work). Do not spray while direct sun is shining on the plant. Small beige trails running through your beet or Swiss chard leaves mean leaf miners. If more than 30 percent of the plant is affected, spray with Sevin at seven-day intervals and wait a week after spraying before harvesting. If you find fusarium and verticillium wilt on your tomato plants, use resistant varieties next season. Write to your cooperative agricultural extension service for a listing of recommended varieties, or check seed catalogs. Don't worry if you see some yellowing of interior tomato leaves. It is perfectly normal this time of the year owing to shading from top growth. Geranium cuttings can be taken year-round if you have a good parent plant.

Liatris, hollyhocks, dahlias, astilbe, annual impatiens or balsam

PLANT	DATE PLANTED	COMMENTS

Purple coneflower
(*Echinacea purpurea*)

PLANT	DATE PLANTED	COMMENTS

Baby Bibb and oakleaf
lettuces, banana sweet peppers,
and onions

Zinnias, roses,
and Gloriosa daisies

PLANT	DATE PLANTED	COMMENTS

Spider flower cleome

PLANT	DATE PLANTED	COMMENTS

Brugmansia

PLANT	DATE PLANTED	COMMENTS

Planting Diagram: Take time while reaping the harvest of your garden to plant biennials: pansies, violas

d Canterbury bells will grow in the fall and bloom next spring and summer.

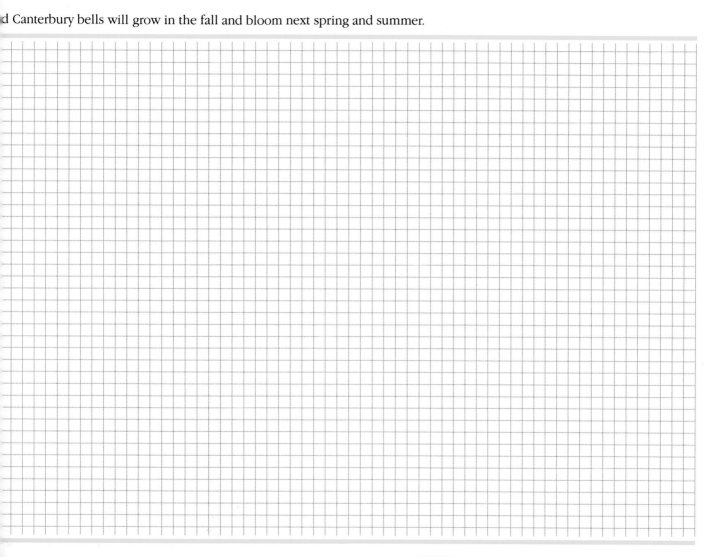

$\mathcal{S}$EPTEMBER signals the beginning of autumn, and as leaves start falling, add them to your compost pile. The resulting leaf mold is excellent for soil improvement and potting. Remember that proper proportions of nitrogen and moisture are necessary to get the pile to "heat up," which occurs most readily if the pile is built in a week or two. The addition of fresh green fodder—cut grass or young tender weeds—and a turning of the pile can usually get the friendly bacteria in a compost pile going quickly.

It should still be possible to plant cool-weather crops: lettuce, spinach, kale, and radishes. In fact, some actually benefit from the cooler temperatures. You might consider putting in new rose plants now. Although they will make little root growth this season, the soil will settle firmly about the roots through the fall, and the plants will be well established and ready to start active growth as soon as the ground and air reach growing temperatures. Most gardeners have far more time to prepare their rose beds properly now than in the busy months of spring.

This is the time to divide daylilies and phlox once they have flowered. Harvest and remove eggplants, tomatoes, corn, peppers, and squash plants. And don't forget to harvest herbs for drying just when the first few flowers open. Pick off 4 or 5 inches of the tender new growth tips, wash in cold water, and pat dry. Tie the shoots loosely in small bunches and hang to dry in a cool, airy spot.

Roses

Tips.

If it has been dry and below 65°F all day, and the temperature drops to 55°F with no wind just before sundown, watch out—frost is likely! As areas of your garden become vacant, sow a cover crop of "green manure" to prevent soil erosion during the winter. Ryegrass is one of the best, another is buckwheat. If your growing season is brief, consider stretching it with plastic tunnels, cloches, or solar growing frames. A solution of nondetergent soap (2 tablespoons of flakes to 1 gallon of water) acts as a mild insecticide against scales and aphids on your houseplants. Sponge the leaves carefully, and don't forget the undersides. Be sure that plants growing in the cold frame get ample water. On frosty evenings cover the frame with 8 to 10 inches of hay. Nature's thermometer: count the number of times a cricket chirps in fifteen seconds, add forty, and you will have the current temperature. Early leaf drop may be due to a dry summer. If so, water trees thoroughly before they go into a dormant condition later in the season. Prevent some of next year's fruit disease problems by gathering up all fallen leaves, twigs, and infected fruit. Keep your plants clean!

Eucomis bicolor

Winter Care for Roses.

How best to protect roses during the harsh winter months is one of the most hotly debated gardening subjects, but the very first rule to learn about rose winterization is that there *are* no hard-and-fast rules. Each garden is different, and various factors of a particular micro-climate help or hinder any plant's ability to winter well and should be considered when deciding where to plant roses, and which varieties to choose.

Rose

There are many different winterization techniques, including protection with plastic foam, cones, wire mesh, cold frames, or straw covered with burlap. All good winterization methods, however, begin with a deep root bed that will assure survival of the plant's root system and bud union (the point at which the branches join the plant's main trunk) all winter long.

One of the easiest and most commonly practiced methods is mounding. Eight to 10 inches of soil that drains easily (taken from another part of the garden) is mounded around the base of the rose plant, then allowed to freeze. Once frozen, the mound should be covered with straw, evergreen boughs, or oak leaves (which won't pack or mat down) retained by wire netting, to keep the mound frozen until spring. For taller rosebushes it may be necessary to dig up one side of the plant's roots so that it can be bent down to the ground, then covered with soil.

Whichever method you choose, winter protection for roses really begins in the summer. Vigorous, healthy plants tolerate the cold better, while diseased, weak roses just can't make it through a freezing winter. So keep your roses in good shape and ease them into dormancy with care.

Aster frikarti

PLANT	DATE PLANTED	COMMENTS

PLANT	DATE PLANTED	COMMENTS

Dahlia

Dahlias

PLANT	DATE PLANTED	COMMENTS

PLANT	DATE PLANTED	COMMENTS

Herb vinegars

CTOBER is a cornucopia of peas, lettuce, broccoli, cauliflower, tomatoes, radishes, pumpkins, leeks, lima beans, and beets. Continue to harvest until the ground freezes. You should also be planting evergreens (which must be soaked with water immediately after planting to prevent winter burning), rhubarb, and shallots this month.

If you do not have a root cellar, carrots, brussels sprouts, parsnips, and Jerusalem artichokes can be left in the garden on into the winter. Just before the soil freezes hard, cover the plants (except kale and sprouts) with an 8- to 10-inch hay mulch. This will keep the soil workable and soft so you can dig out your crop as needed. Sprouts and kale can endure extreme cold and even improve in taste! Just snap off sprouts (from the bottom of the plant up) and leaves and cook before they thaw.

As a rule, there is no frost until around October 15 in most of the East and Midwest, but you should begin taking in houseplants that have summered outdoors (checking first for insects) and pruning if necessary. Begonias, fuchsias, lantanas, and geraniums should be dug up, potted, and brought in. You can put cold frames to work, wintering tender plants, protecting crops of radishes and baby lettuce, or even forcing daffodil, tulip, and hyacinth bulbs.

Fall berries and dahlias

Pumpkins

Tips.

Daffodils, tulips, and hyacinths need 8 to 10 weeks in cold storage to form a good root system. An extra refrigerator or root cellar can be used to store pots of bulbs for forcing later. Learn to read weather signs, especially in the autumn. For example, clear days with deep blue skies may signal a frost. Gather all the mature ears on your cornstalks and save them for the squirrels. Run the stalks through a shredder and put the scraps in the compost pile. Store white potatoes in covered bags or boxes so light can't reach them and turn the skins green. The greenish part of potatoes can cause stomachache. When potting tulips for forcing, place bulbs so the flat side of the bulb is toward the edge of the pot. The leaves will form out from this side and hide the bare stems. Cooling soil makes October the best time to harvest horseradish. Spring planting will avoid a tangle of roots, so save some of the pencil-thin roots for a new crop. Continue to water roses, for they may bloom well into November. Cut all the tall, whippy branches to prevent wind damage, but wait until March for the more serious annual pruning.

Apples

Bulb Planting.

Many of the bulbs that will announce next year's spring do best if planted right now, just before the ground freezes, while others prefer the milder temperatures of spring planting. Here is a list of the most popular bulb flowers, the best planting season for each, and the proper depth for planting. Whenever you plant bulbs, be sure they get plenty of sunshine while in the leaf-producing stage.

Hardy chrysanthemums
and cosmos

NAME	WHEN TO PLANT	PLANTING DEPTH (INCHES)
Anemone	Plant now	3
Begonia	Wait until spring	2
Bleeding heart	Plant now	3
Calla lily	Wait until spring	4
Canna	Wait until spring	6
Crocus	Plant now	4
Daffodil	Plant now	6
Dahlia	Wait until spring	7
Freesia	Plant now or spring	2
Gladiolus	Wait until spring	4
Hyacinth and grape hyacinth	Plant now	4–6
Iris (bearded, Dutch)	Plant now	2–4
Lily (all varieties)	Plant now	6–7
Lily of the valley	Plant now	1
Narcissus	Plant now	5
Peony	Plant now	2
Ranunculus	Plant now or spring	2
Tuberose	Wait until spring	4
Tulip	Plant now	6–7

PLANT	DATE PLANTED	COMMENTS

Etain rose

Japanese anemones and
a lavender-pink chrysanthemum

PLANT	DATE PLANTED	COMMENTS

PLANT	DATE PLANTED	COMMENTS

PLANT	DATE PLANTED	COMMENTS

Rhubarb chard
in pine needle mulch

Bulb Planting Diagram: Plant your bulbs now for spring bloom, and don't forget to mulch after

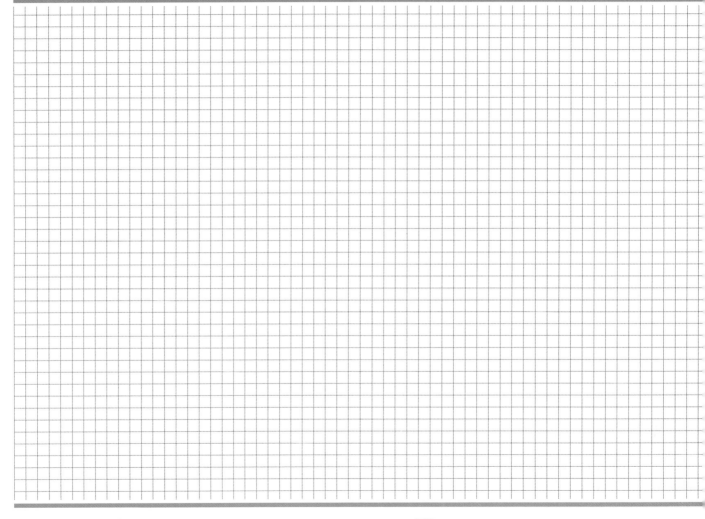

the first freeze-up.

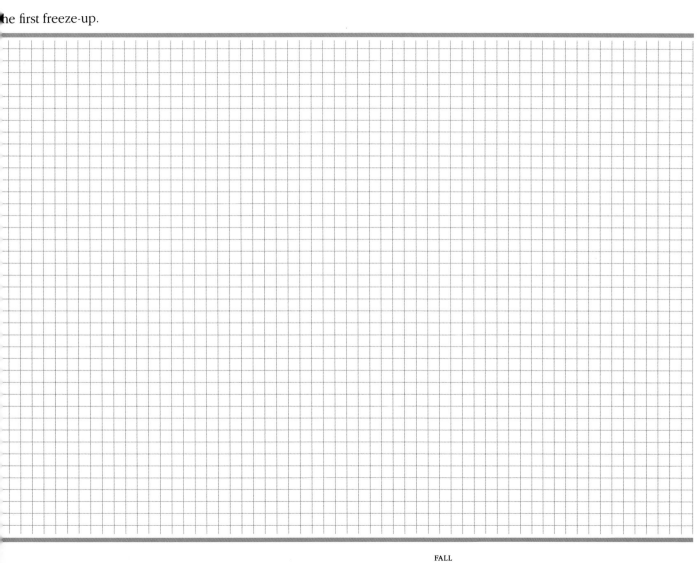

NOVEMBER ushers in the holidays, which I call the fifth season because they have a flavor and excitement all their own. Although your gardens will not be as active now as they are during the summer months, there is plenty to do in preparation for the coming year.

The first priority for this month is winterizing the garden so that it will be in good shape for the next season. Clear all remaining plant refuse from the garden and add it to the leaves you've raked up in the compost heap. Shallow tilling is an excellent way to destroy insect eggs by exposing them to the sun, weather, birds, and other predators. Your garden must be put to bed spic-and-span if it is to be prepared for next spring's plantings.

Fall applications of slow-growth fertilizer should be made on dormant shrubs and trees; this is easily accomplished after the leaves have fallen. Since the soil is still relatively warm (above 40°F), the roots will absorb the nutrients more readily now than they will in early spring.

When the frost is on the pumpkin, make sure your precooled bulbs have been planted. Fragrant paper-white narcissus are a good choice. Set narcissus bulbs in shallow bowls of pebbles and water, and put in a dark place with a temperature of about 50°F to root; after two or three weeks bring to a stronger light. When flower shoots are 6 to 7 inches high, bring to a bright window, but not into direct sunlight. You'll have a glorious display for the holidays in about five weeks!

Once the soil has frozen hard, it's a good idea to mulch beds of perennials and bulbs with 4 to 6 inches of a light material like straw or evergreen branches. Put your garden to bed as you would your child. Your plants will thank you next spring.

Strawflowers

Mulched beds of peonies
with winter rye

Thanksgiving and Christmas require lots of preparation. Your garden should be an endless source of inspiration for decorating. Take a walk in your yard or in the woods and see what you can find. Dried cornstalks, pumpkins, gourds, colorful autumn leaves, pine cones, garlands of evergreens, and Christmas wreaths will bring the outdoors into your home and make the fifth season bright and festive.

Tips. Guard young fruit trees from gnawing rodents with a protective barrier made from mesh wire or tree guards, which are available in garden stores. When harvesting pumpkins and winter squash, remember to leave 4 to 5 inches of stem attached. Store them on boards or wooden shelves—never touching—and in a cool, dark, dry place. Artemisia, strawflowers, yarrow, and honesty will dry beautifully if hung in a dark, dry place for two weeks. Combined with small branches of beech, leucothoe, or bayberry that have been soaked in a 33 percent glycerine-and-water solution for six days, they make a lovely, lasting bouquet. If the buds fall off your Thanksgiving or Christmas cactus, it's likely that the room is too hot and dry and the plant is suffering from lack of water.

Aster frikarti

Spider chrysanthemums

PLANT	DATE PLANTED	COMMENTS

PLANT	DATE PLANTED	COMMENTS

PLANT	DATE PLANTED	COMMENTS

Ardisia japonica

Evergreen boughs
and pine cones

C. Z. Guest's dining room

*d*ECEMBER'S cold winds, ice, and snow make most plants vulnerable. Protect them with burlap screens and a thick blanket of leaves. This will keep rhododendrons, evergreens, and perennials and biennials from becoming dehydrated due to excessive exposure to sun. Remember, water cannot reach the roots of plants when the ground is frozen.

This is a good time to get your gardening tools and workspace into prime condition for next spring. Sharpen the blades of pruners, saws, and axes so they'll be ready for winter pruning; empty liquids from tank sprayers, flush them with clean water, and drain; winterize the engines of the power mower, chain saw, and shredder, and wipe all metal parts with an oily rag to prevent rust. You might also want to paint the wooden handles of your garden tools a bright color so they'll be easier to spot outside. And store empty, washed plastic and clay pots outdoors; the winter freezing will automatically sterilize them and keep them ready for use again next spring.

Of course, much of this month should be devoted to holiday activities: making your own wreaths, tree decorations, and fragrant pomander balls, and caring for poinsettias, Christmas cactuses, kalanchoes, and other favorite holiday plants. Many of the plants growing in the garden and woods have attractive seed pods, foliage, or fruit that can be used for Christmas decorations.

Tips.

"Squiggly" packing foam "peanuts" make great drainage material for potted plants, especially for hanging planters, because they're lightweight, do not retain water, and are free. For homemade potpourri, mix 1 quart of fir needles, 1 cup of dried citrus peels, 1 cup of rosemary, 1 cup of dried basil, 2 to 4 crumbled bay leaves, and 2 cups of coarse salt. Delightfully fragrant pomander balls—limes, lemons, or oranges studded with cloves, sometimes rolled in a mixture of aromatic spices—are perfect for scenting a room or perfuming a linen closet. They make inexpensive small presents that last indefinitely. Check Christmas-tree sales after the twenty-fifth; many dealers will give away unsold trees. They are perfect for bird shelters and, when brittle and dry, make good kindling. Old Christmas wreaths make great mulch-retaining rings when placed around azaleas, blueberry bushes, and other small acid-loving shrubs, and their nutrients will eventually decompose into the soil. Garden tools and gadgets make wonderful Christmas presents. If you have a friend who "has everything," think about a birdbath or birdhouse for his or her feathered friends.

Paper white narcissi
and holly wreath

Choosing a Christmas Tree.

What would Christmas be without the sight and smell of a beautifully trimmed tree? This charming custom came from England, where the tradition was borrowed from German religious plays featuring a lovely *Christbaum,* or wreath, decorated with roses, wafers, and apples.

There are about 40 different types of Christmas trees, but the most popular are white pine, fir, spruce, and Scotch pine.

Here are some pointers to keep in mind when selecting a fresh Christmas tree: ▲ Naturally, shape is important. The traditional Christmas tree tapers from a broad, bushy base to a spiral top. ▲ The tree should be a healthy green color with no brown patches and should exude the fresh fragrance of evergreen. Red pine, white pine, and Scotch pine, Douglas fir, balsam fir, and white fir are best for needle retention and longevity. ▲ To test for freshness, gently bend the needles back; if they break, the tree is too dry. Run your hand across the bottom of the stump. Usually it will be wet and sticky if the tree has been freshly cut. ▲ When you are ready to bring the tree inside, place it in a stand that has a well for water. Never let the container run dry! Water helps replace the moisture given off by needles in a warm room. ▲ If you choose a living tree, or an uncut tree that has been dug and burlapped, remember to dig a hole for it before the ground freezes and cover the hole with insulating material, such as straw or leaves. Do not keep it in the house for more than a few days, and then place it in a cool basement or garage to harden off before transplanting. A direct transfer from a warm house to freezing temperatures outside can kill a tree. Proper planting will have to wait until the ground thaws in spring.

Christmas tree

Dwarf myrtle tied with raffia

PLANT	DATE PLANTED	COMMENTS

PLANT	DATE PLANTED	COMMENTS

Orchid

Favorite Suppliers by Category

GENERAL

Wayside Gardens
Hodges, SC 29695
(800) 845-1124

BULBS

Ralph Cook
(914) 796-3492 (Westchester County, NY)
(407) 798-5513 (Palm Beach County, FL)

CHRYSANTHEMUMS

King's Mums
P.O. Box 368
Clements, CA 95227
(209) 759-3571

GREENHOUSES

Hobby Greenhouse Association
Glen Terrace
Bedford, MA 01730

National Greenhouse Manufacturers Association
6 Honey Bee Lane
P.O. Box 1350
Taylors, SC 29687
(803) 244-3854

HOUSEPLANTS, HERBS, PERENNIALS

Logee's Greenhouses
141 North St.
Danielson, CT 06239
(203) 774-8038

ORCHIDS

Alberts & Merkel Bros., Inc.
2210 S. Federal Highway
Boynton Beach, FL 33435
(407) 732-2071

ROSES

Jackson & Perkins
P.O. Box 1028
Medford, OR 97501
(800) 872-7673

SEEDS (FLOWER, FRUIT, AND VEGETABLE)

W. Atlee Burpee Seed Company
300 Park Ave.
Warminster, PA 18991
(215) 674-4915

The Cook's Garden
P.O. Box 535
Londonderry, VT 05148
(802) 824-3400

Gurney's Seed & Nursery Co.
Yankton, SD 57079
(605) 665-1671

Geo. W. Park Seed Co., Inc.
Greenwood, SC 29647
(800) 845-3369

Ronnigers Seed Potatoes
Star Route
Moysie Springs, ID 83845